It's Easy To Play New Chart Hits

All This Time (Michelle), 2
Breathe Easy (Blue), 7
Changes (Kelly & Ozzy Osbourne), 12
The Closest Thing To Crazy (Katie Melua), 17
Cry (Alex Parks), 20
Leave Right Now (Will Young), 24
Mad World (Michael Andrews featuring Gary Jules), 29
Red Blooded Woman (Kylie Minogue), 32
Somewhere Only We Know (Keane), 37
Take Me Out (Franz Ferdinand), 42

Published by
Wise Publications
8/9 Frith Street, London W1D 3JB, England.

Exclusive Distributors:
Music Sales Limited
Distribution Centre, Newmarket Road, Bury St Edmunds, Suffolk IP33 3YB, England.
Music Sales Pty Limited
120 Rothschild Avenue, Rosebery, NSW 2018, Australia.

Order No. AM89676
ISBN 0-7119-3054-6
This book © Copyright 2004 by Wise Publications.

Unauthorised reproduction of any part of this publication by
any means including photocopying is an infringement of copyright.

Music arranged by Carlton Edwards.
Music processed by Paul Ewers Music Design.
Cover photographs courtesy London Features International.
Printed in the United Kingdom by Caligraving Limited, Thetford, Norfolk.

Your Guarantee of Quality
As publishers, we strive to produce every book to the highest commercial standards.
The music has been freshly engraved and the book has been carefully designed to
minimise awkward page turns and to make playing from it a real pleasure.
Particular care has been given to specifying acid-free, neutral-sized paper made from
pulps which have not been elemental chlorine bleached.
This pulp is from farmed sustainable forests and was produced with special regard for the environment.
Throughout, the printing and binding have been planned to ensure a sturdy,
attractive publication which should give years of enjoyment.
If your copy fails to meet our high standards, please inform us and we will gladly replace it.

www.musicsales.com

This publication is not authorised for sale in
the United States of America and / or Canada

Wise Publications
part of The Music Sales Group

London / New York / Paris / Sydney / Copenhagen / Berlin / Madrid / Tokyo

All This Time

Words & Music by Wayne Hector, Steve Mac & Lorne Tennant

© Copyright 2003 Universal Music Publishing Limited (33.33%)/
Chrysalis Music Limited (33.33%)/Rokstone Music Limited (33.34%).
All Rights Reserved. International Copyright Secured.

Breathe Easy

Words & Music by Lee Ryan, Lars Jensen & Martin Larsson

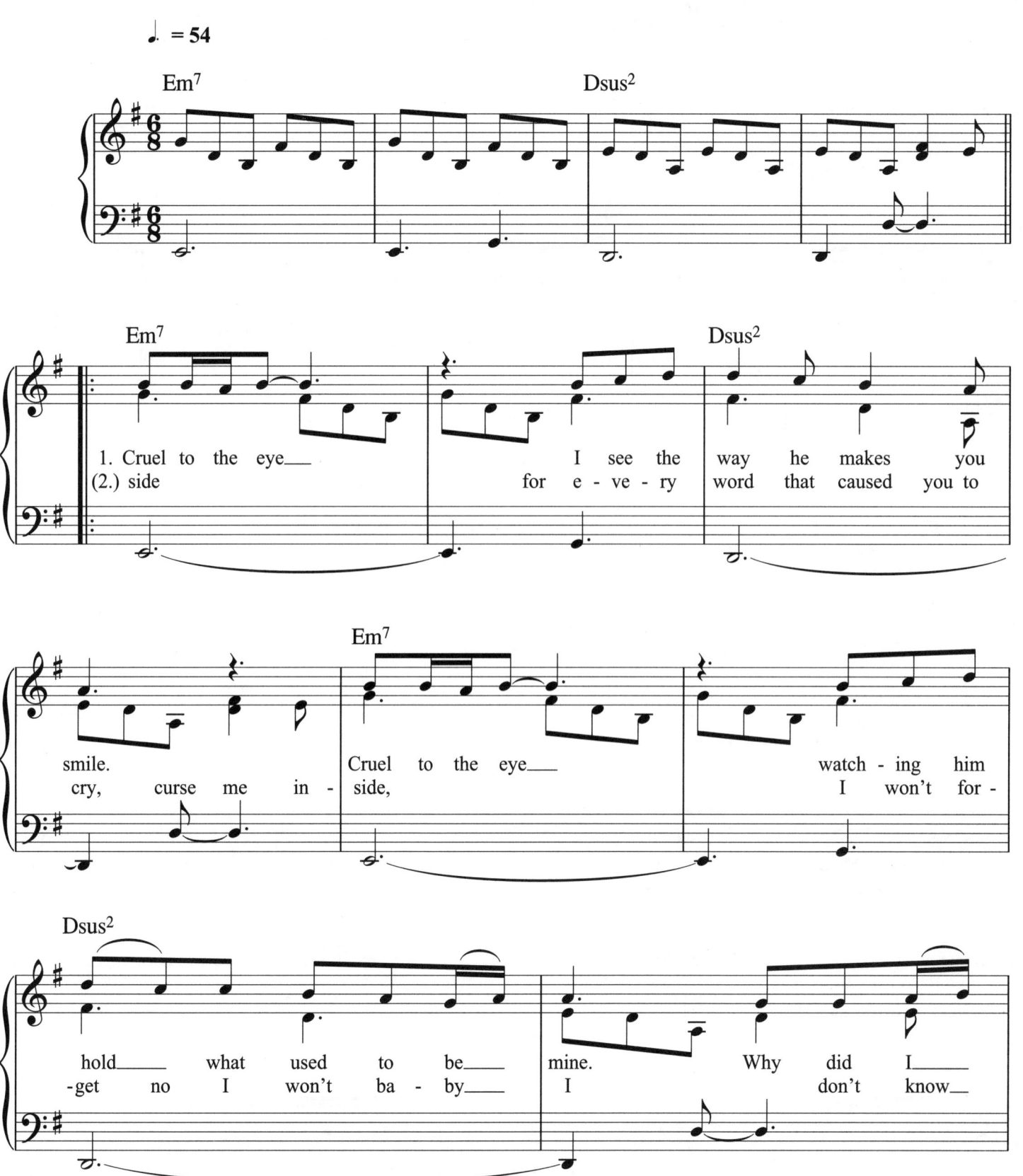

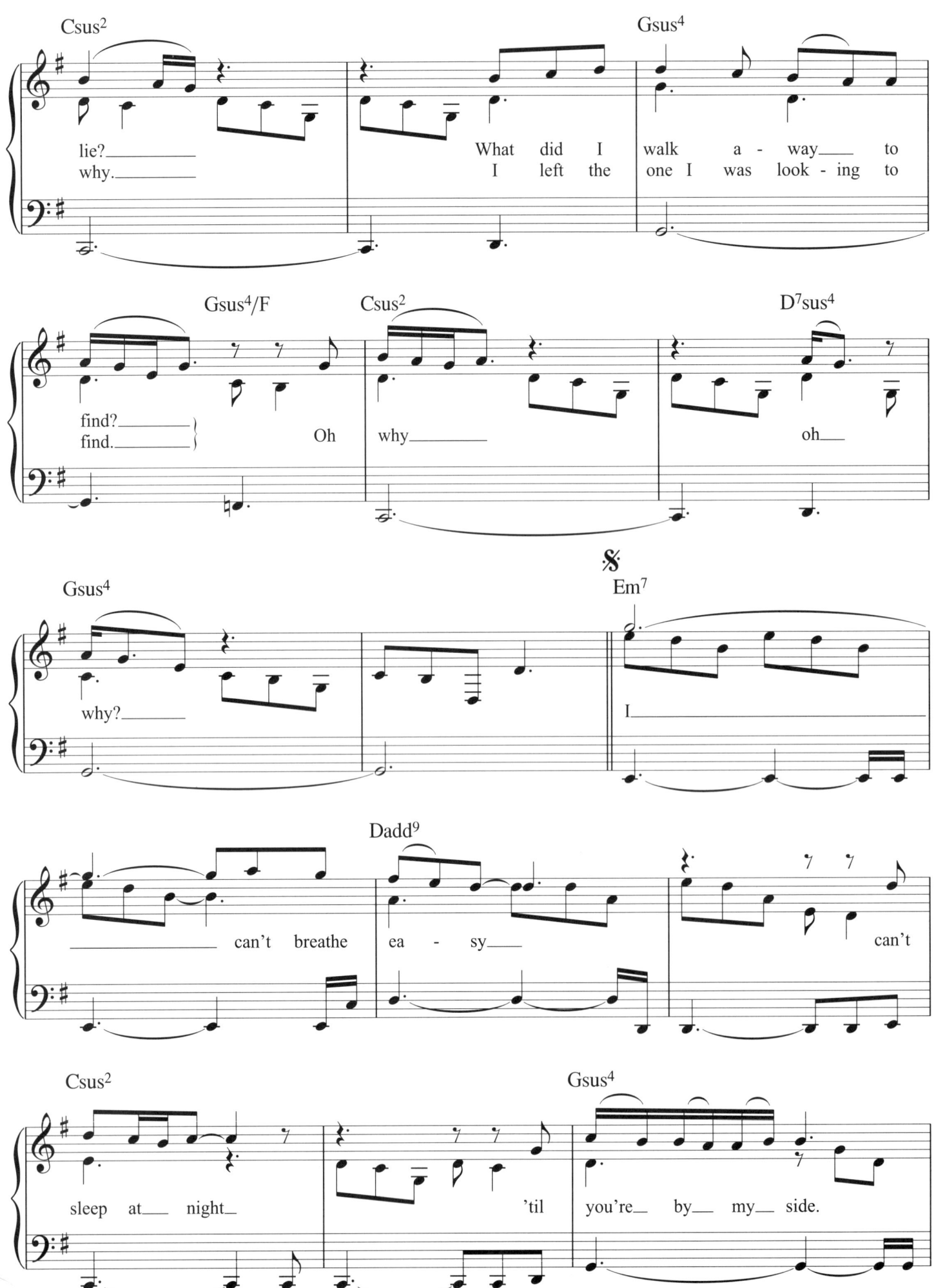

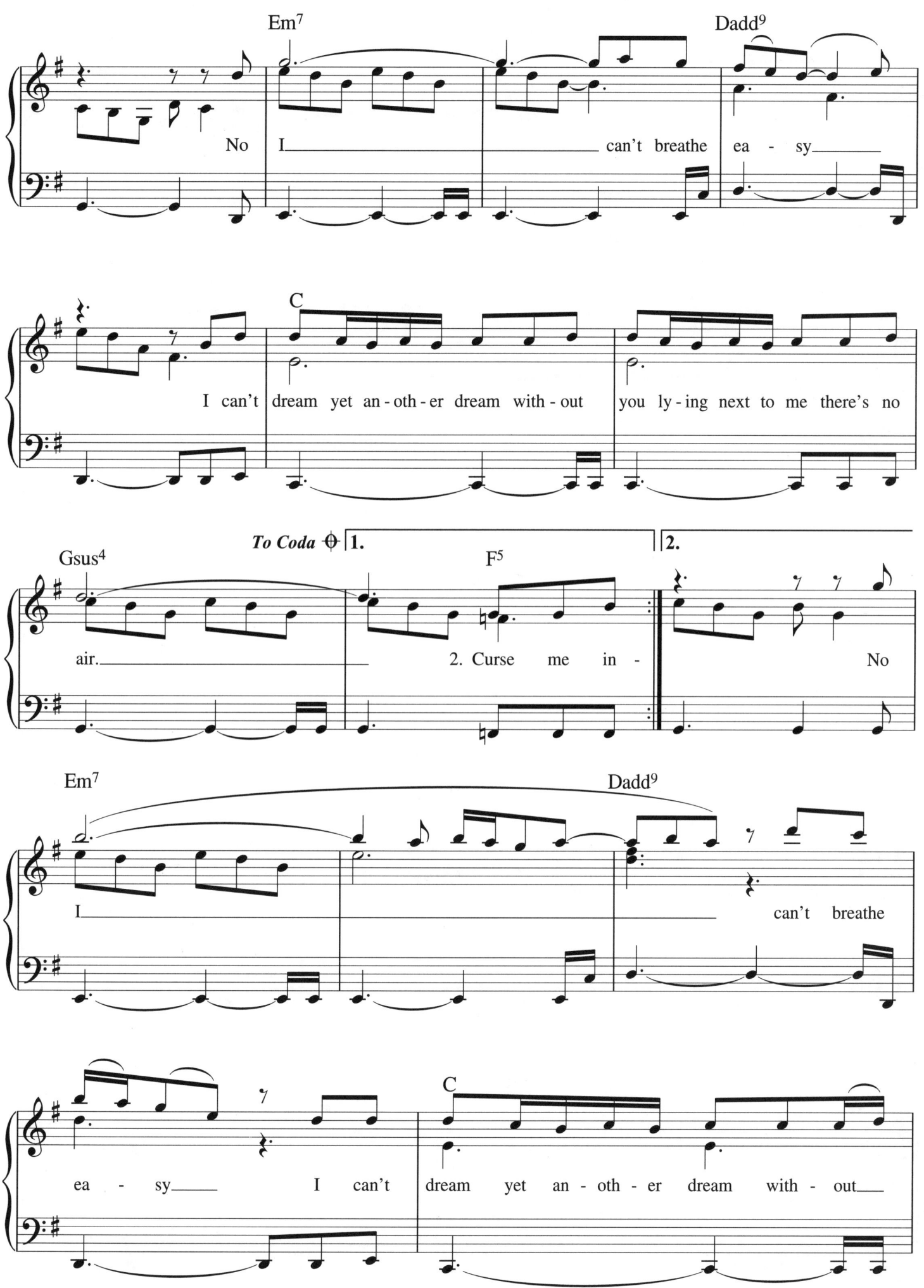

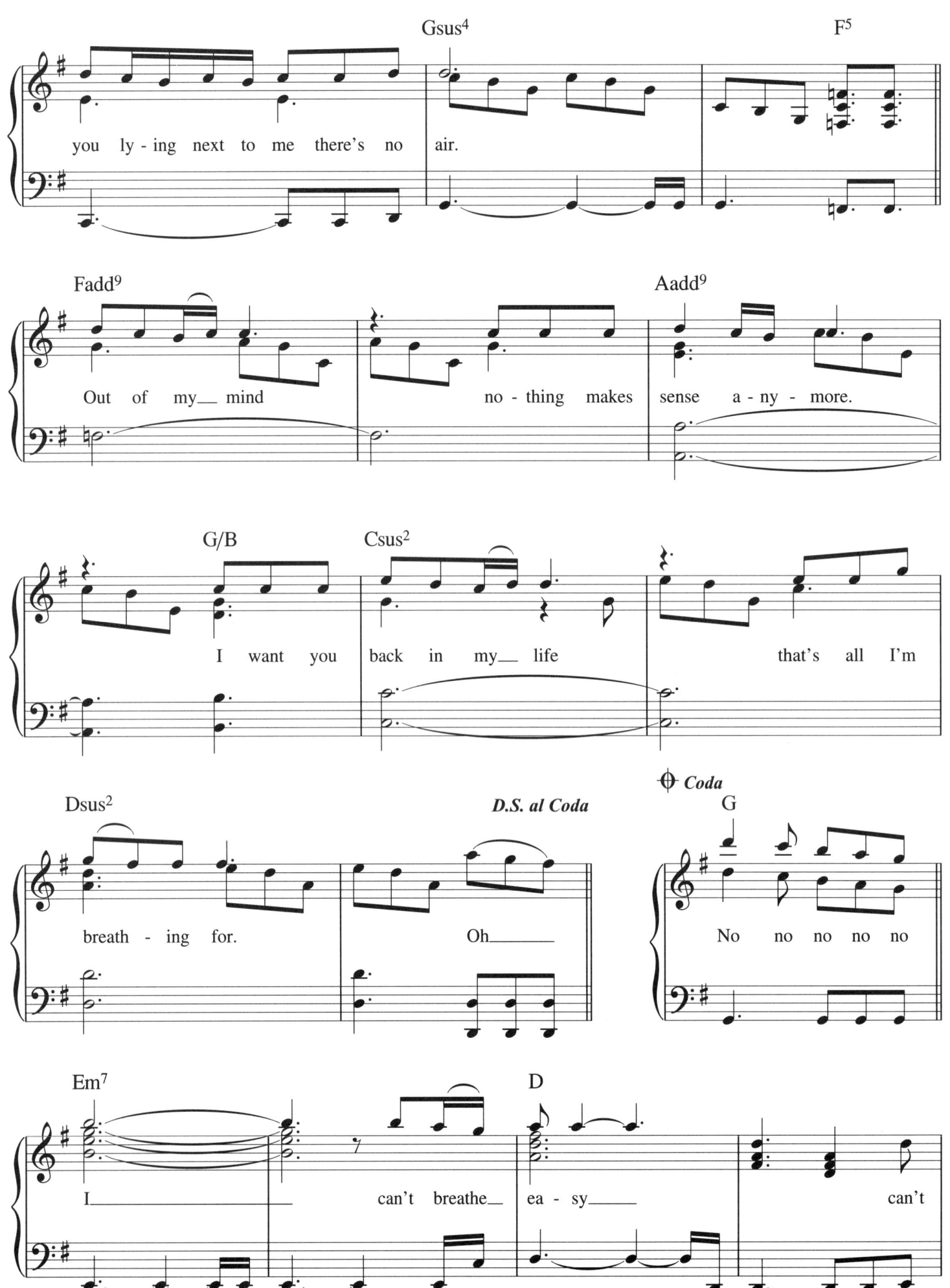

Changes

Words & Music by Ozzy Osbourne, Terence Butler, Terry Iommi & William Ward

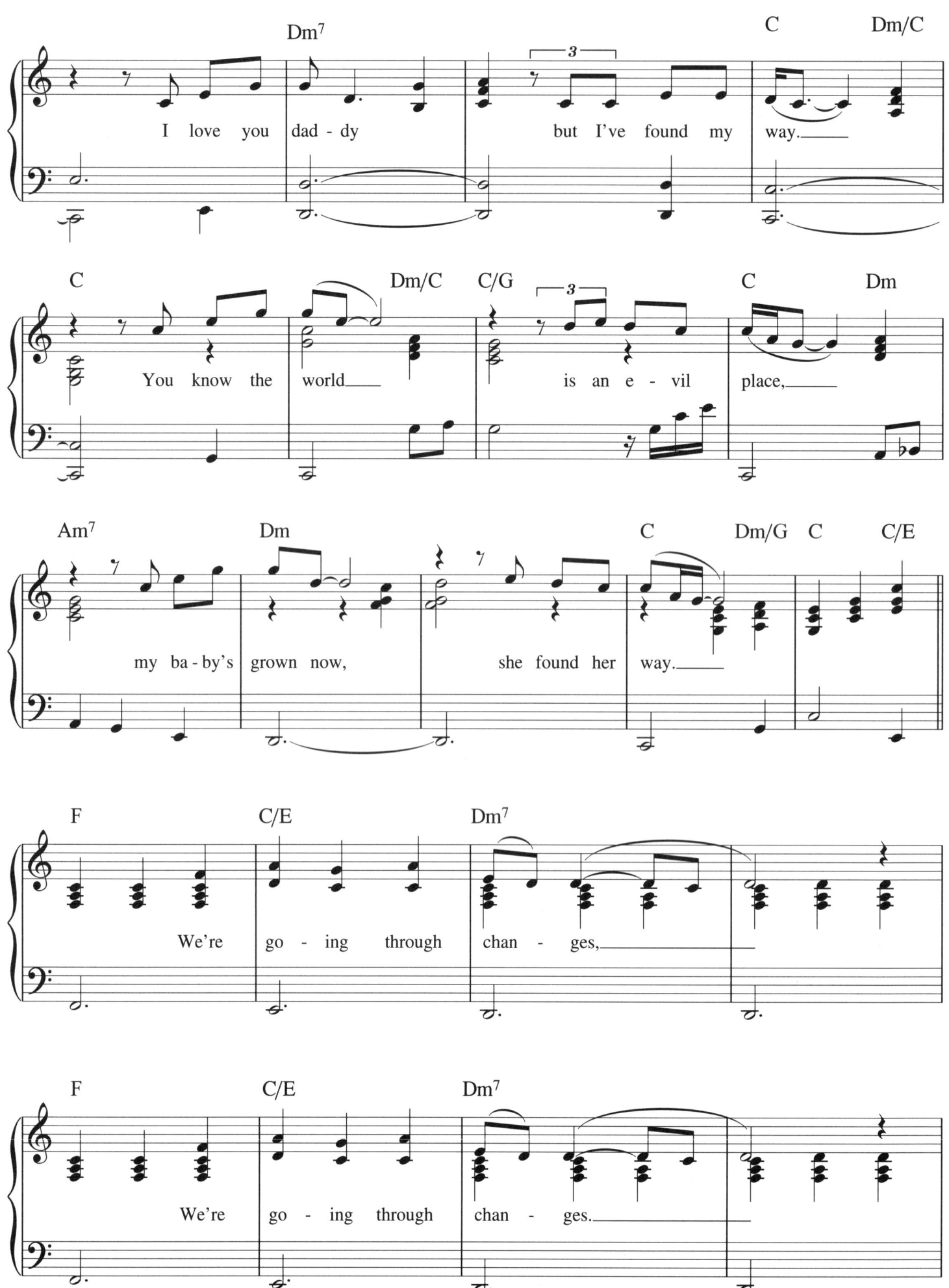

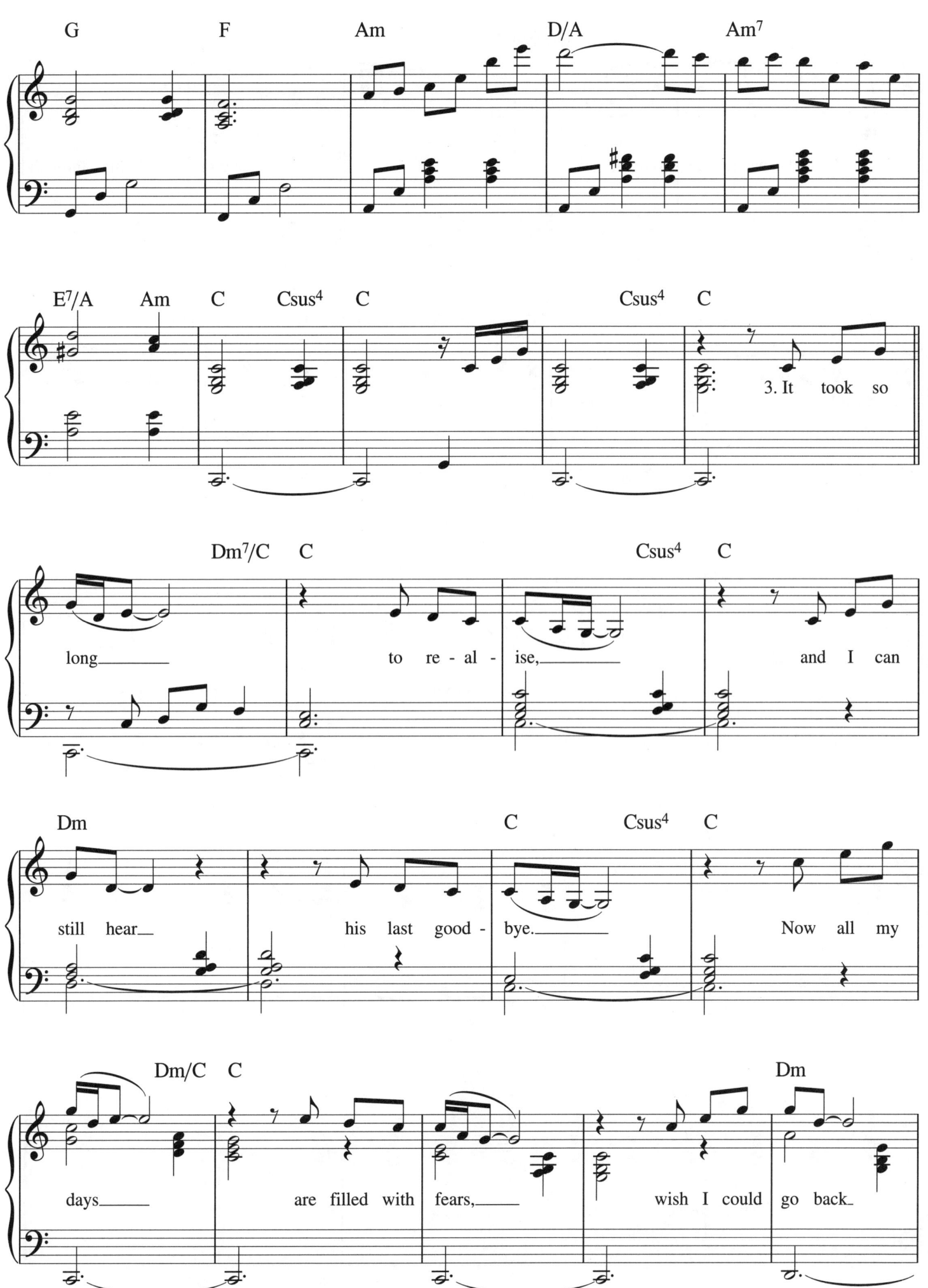

The Closest Thing To Crazy

Words & Music by Mike Batt

Cry

Words & Music by Gary Clark, Alex Parks & Mark Hewardine

© Copyright 2003 Chrysalis Music Limited (66.66%)/Copyright Control (33.34%).
All Rights Reserved. International Copyright Secured.

Leave Right Now

Words & Music by Francis White

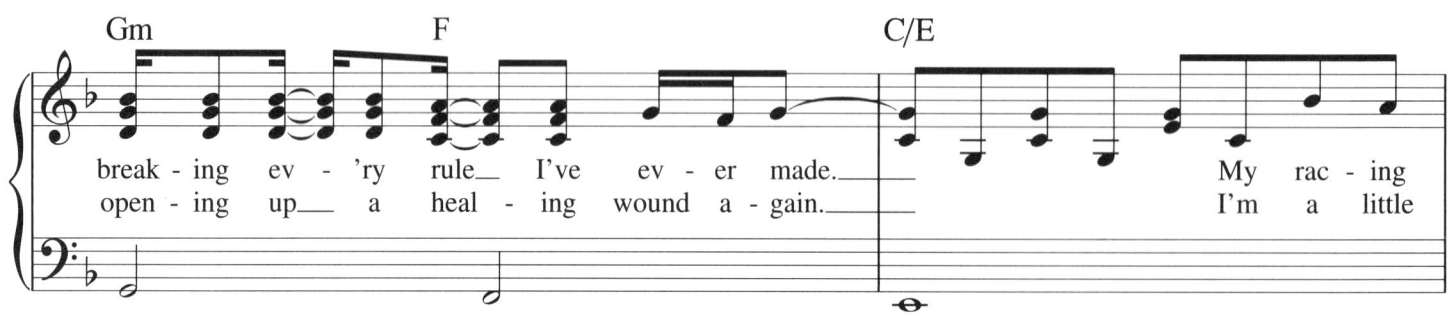
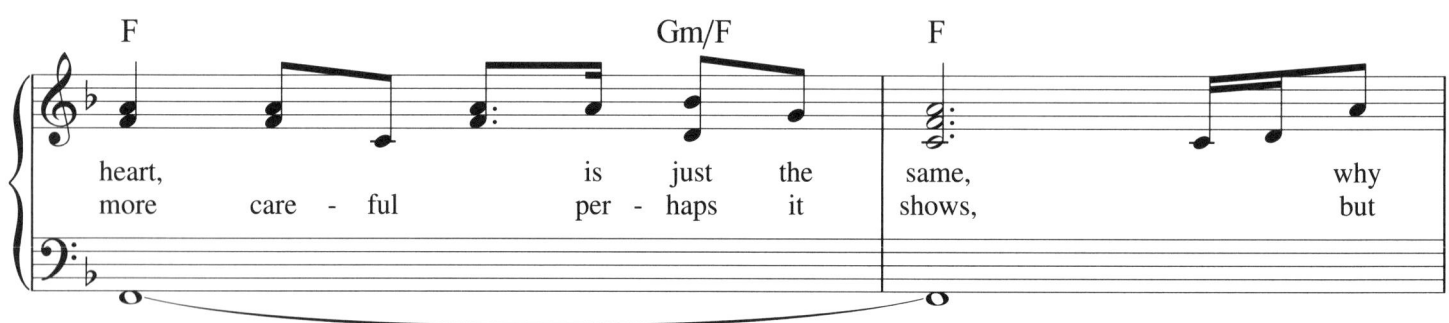

© Copyright 2003 Universal Music Publishing Limited.
All Rights Reserved. International Copyright Secured.

Mad World

Words & Music by Roland Orzabal

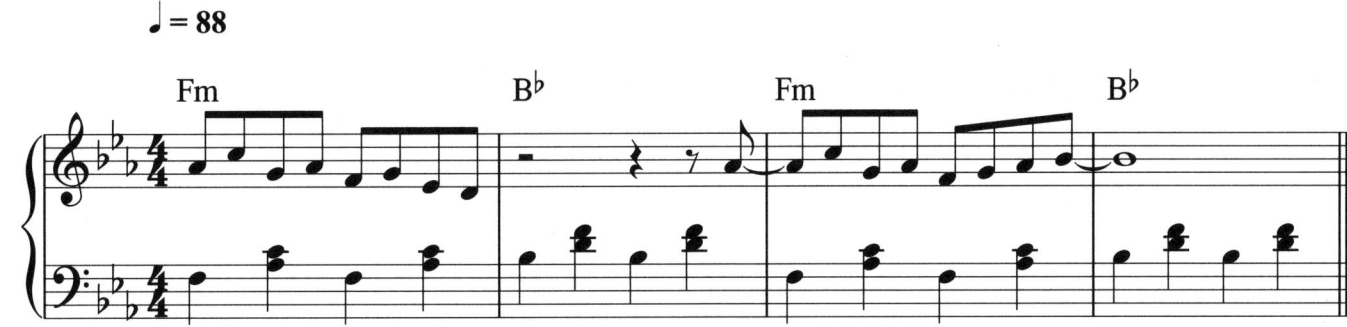

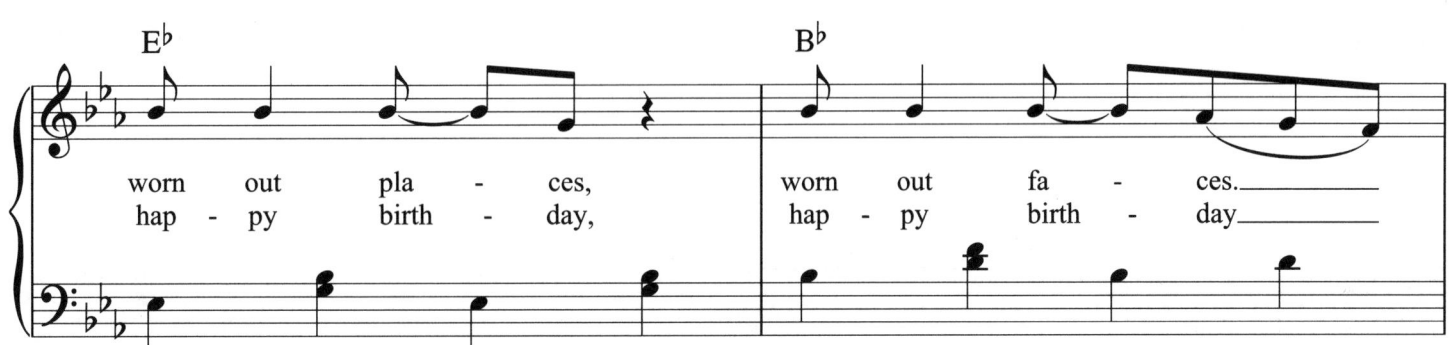
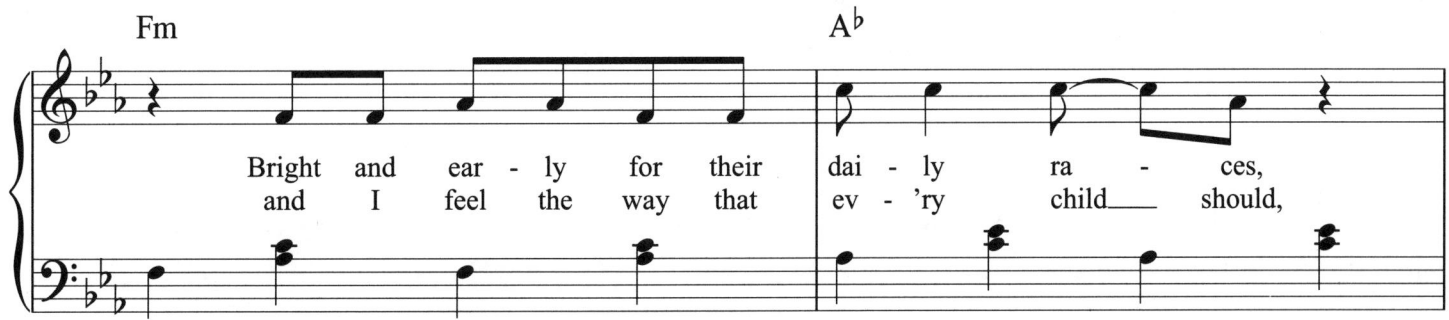

© Copyright 1982 Roland Orzabal Limited. Chrysalis Music Limited.
All Rights Reserved. International Copyright Secured.

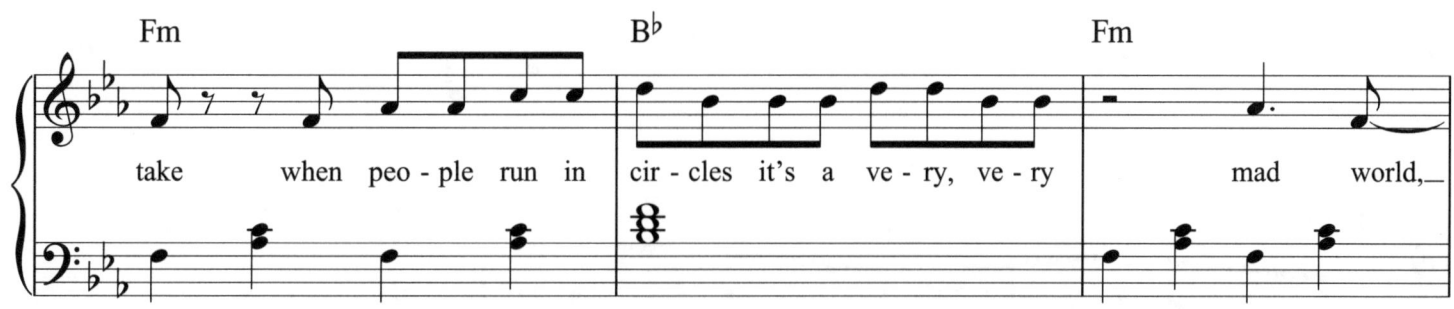
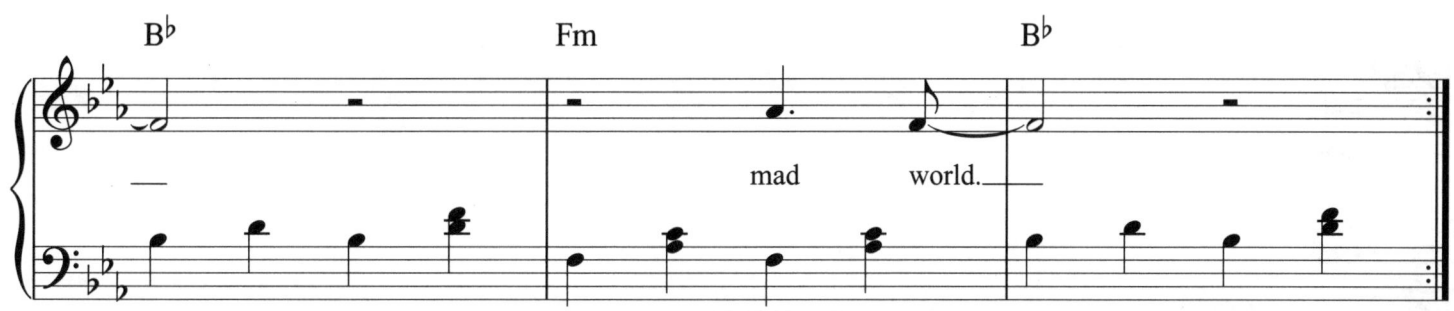

Red Blooded Woman

Words & Music by Jonathan Douglas & Karen Poole

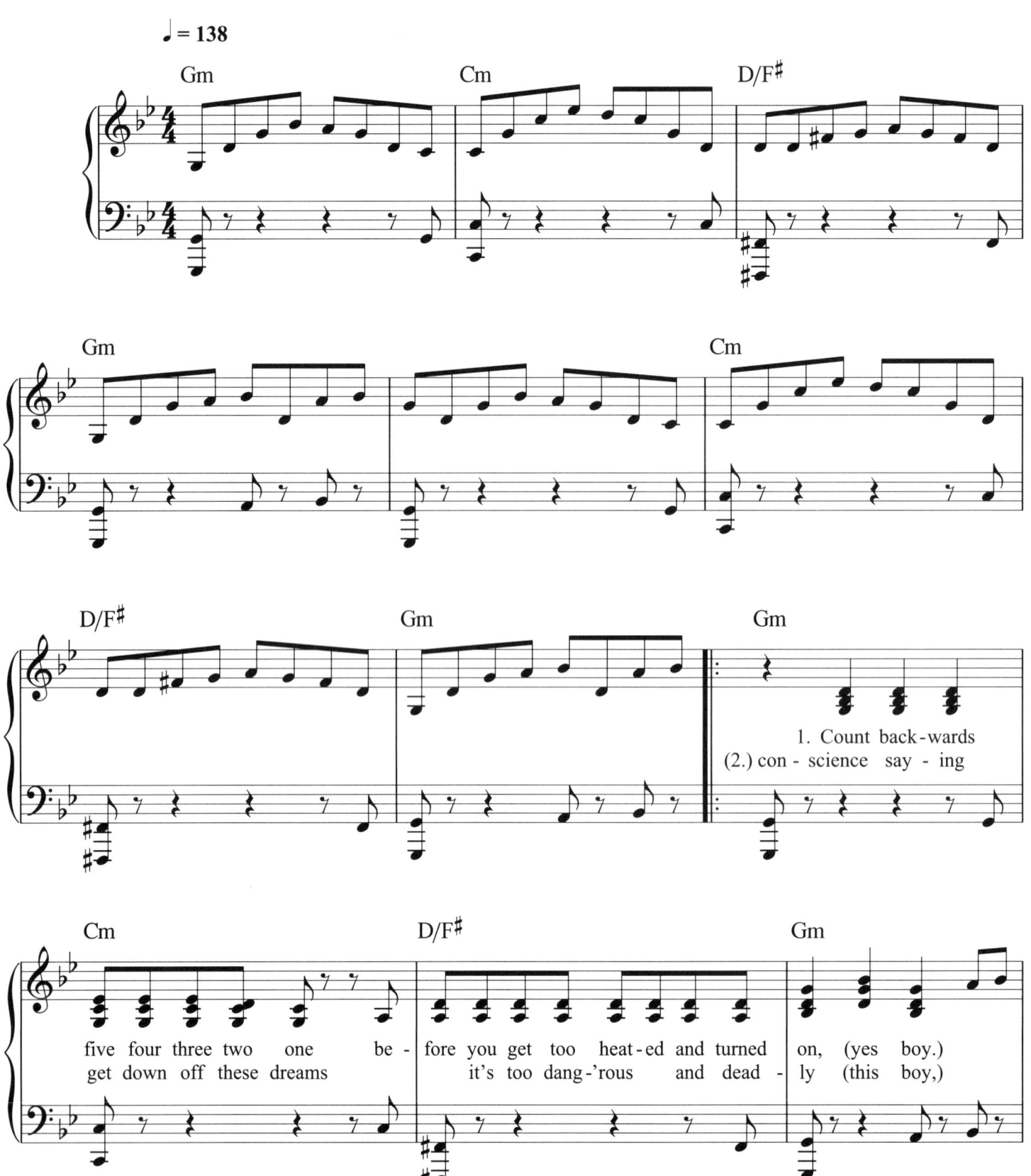

Somewhere Only We Know

Words & Music by Tim Rice-Oxley, Tom Chaplin & Richard Hughes

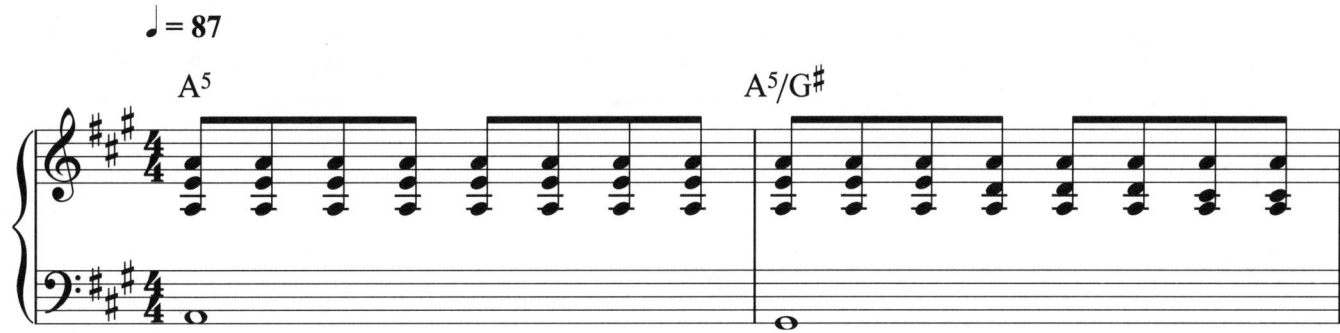

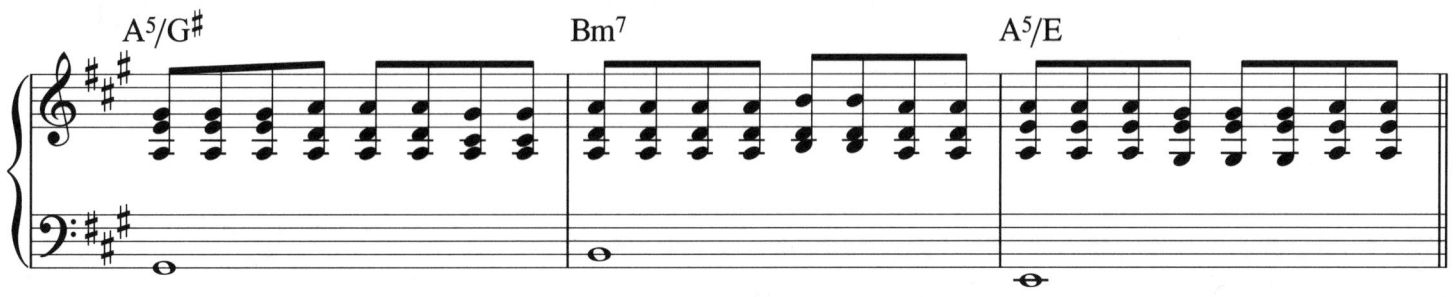
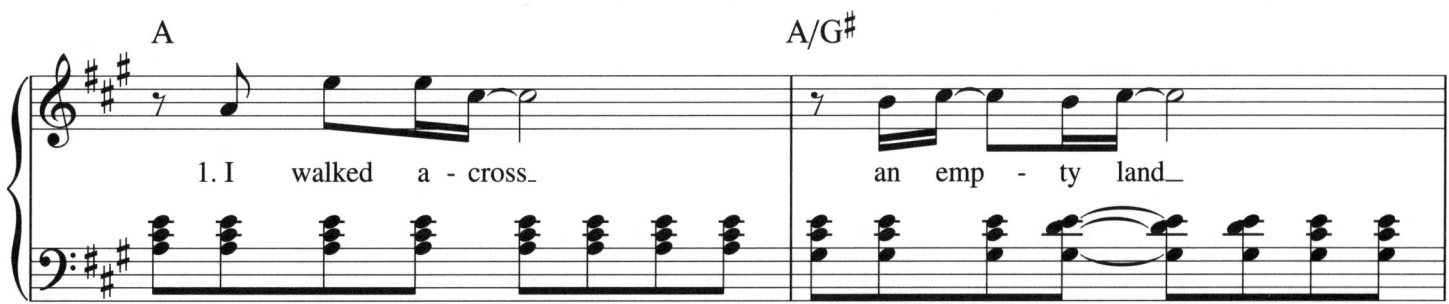

© Copyright 2004 BMG Music Publishing Limited.
All Rights Reserved. International Copyright Secured.

37

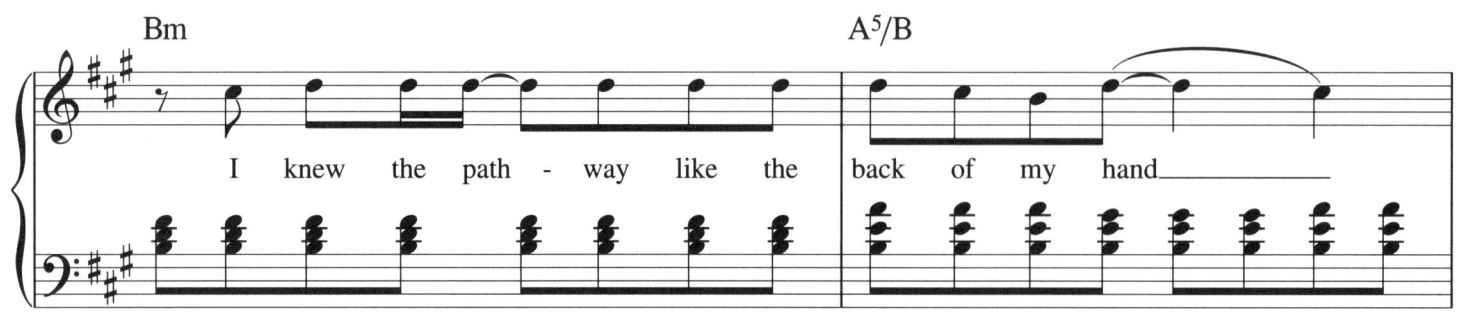

Take Me Out

Words & Music by Alexander Kapranos & Nicholas McCarthy

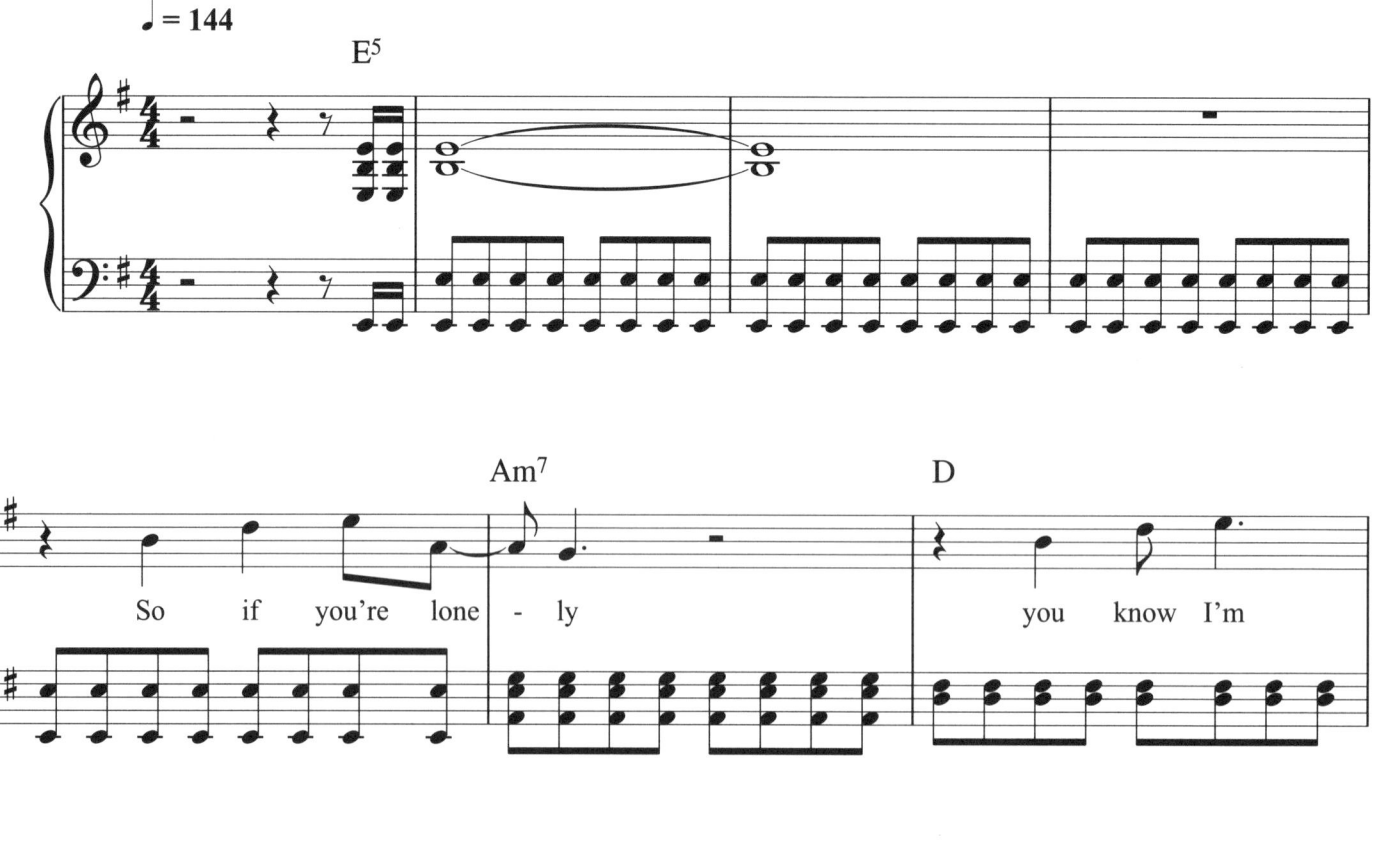

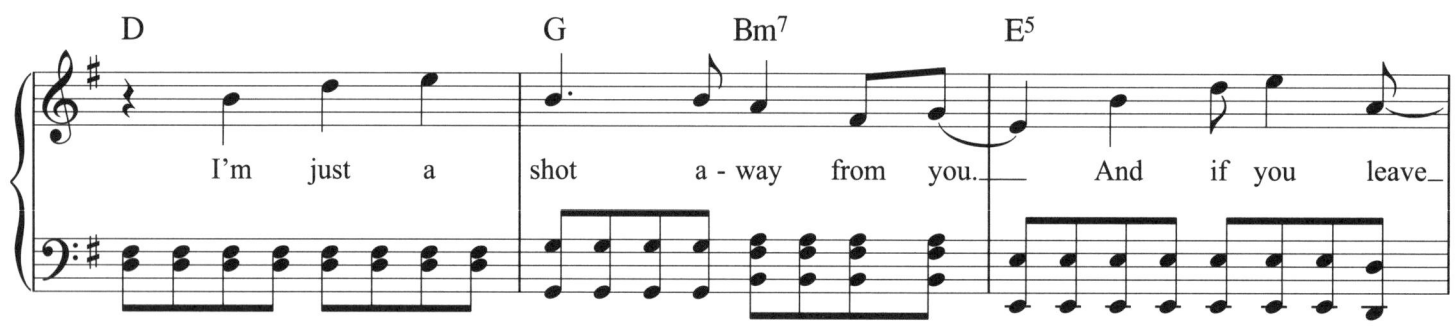

© Copyright 2004 Universal Music Publishing Limited.
All Rights Reserved. International Copyright Secured.